I0017715

Advanced Hacks

for Twitch

Content

The streaming trend is one of the most preferred modalities nowadays, since it is a more interactive form or presentation of content, the best proposal of this kind of content is found through Twitch, this is an interesting platform that increasingly adds more features to make each account shine.

The service and the options offered by this platform for each account is something you should know, either to enjoy each entertainment alternative or to form an account with which you can make your user recognized and at the same time generate money, so you are going to have the most basic and advanced data of this medium.

The emergence of Twitch

Twitch's trajectory began in 2011, from that moment it began a successful path, beyond the fact that it was a secondary streaming option behind YouTube, then over time it gained a much more prominent place among users, especially with the support of Amazon, which acquired this platform after its evolution.

It is defined as a video game platform, because being an ideal space for streaming, more and more gamers create a channel on Twitch, especially because there is a lot of content to exploit on a game or any other subject, so today it is still feasible to create and grow an account.

This streaming service gains a wide power of popularity even over children, the origins of the platform have a lot to do with boosting streaming for all kinds of purpose be it for a blog, music, cooking and so on, although the best known subject matter is video games.

Twitch's advantage comes through e-sports, since e-sports was one of the first content offerings that were increasingly consolidated to this current point, making it an ideal space for broadcasts of video game games, regardless of genre.

Twitch itself, in addition to its streamings, shined for including direct chat, so that streamers can maintain feedback as they develop the broadcast, creating a bond with users or fans in real time, thus emitting the feeling of being heard or attended, to create a link between streamer and fan.

The formation of Twitch was part of an offering from Justin.tv, which is a service with great similarity to YouTube, but its forte was on live streaming, because the other services in this category only stream videos on a delayed basis, but in 2014

Justin.tv changed its organization to just be Twitch Interactive.

That kind of change was a response to the enormous popularity and the amount of traffic that Twitch broadcasts, that same year the platform managed to be among the first four platforms with the highest level of online traffic, causing it to reach 50 million unique visits on a monthly basis.

In view of this phenomenon is that the interest of Amazon is awakened, to the point of buying the platform, this financial operation is estimated at 800 million euros, since that purchase Twitch has continued to grow, at the same level that increased visits in the same way functions were added.

One of the new features is that users can offer tips to the streamers they wish, in addition to creating and promoting paid content for the community of Premium users, thus positioning itself as a recognized streaming service in 202, surpassing YouTube Gaming and leaving it aside.

The viewing opportunity provided by Twitch is genuine, as daily it can aggregate up to 15 million users looking to view one of the 3.8 million channels, so creating an account on this platform is an important window to offer content of this level.

Learn how to access Twitch

If you want to be part of Twitch, the first thing you must do is log in to the website or use their applications either for a mobile device or a console, also this platform allows you to view content without registering, but to participate in the chat with the streamers if you need to have an account.

The advantages of a Twitch account are essential, especially because you can receive notifications when they are going to broadcast some live and is a favorite streamer, so creating your own channel is a good decision to consider, you should know that this is a free process and you just have to put a username, password, birth data and email.

- **Find out how to find channels on Twitch**

By logging into Twitch you can get a lot of interesting channels, through the main page or section will emerge the categories that are trending at the time, usually the dominant category is the video game, within which highlights Genshin, League of Legends and Rust.

Each season or innovation of these games is used by specialized streamers on that subject, if you do not want to view any of these categories you can click on "Explore" to know a wide directory of topics, because beyond the games there is also a good offer of content.

One of the most curious or frequented categories is that of users chatting or discussing a topic, some accounts even create a fixed schedule to present their interviews as a kind of newscast or debate that users expect, it is a much more interactive way compared to a radio or podcast.

The topics are treated or presented to the rhythm of the chat, on the other hand, you can discover what the world of Twitch offers, where the accounts that narrate trips or are part of this theme also shine, these are direct that seek to share experiences, this is a sign that not everything is gaming content.

Another interesting category is Talk shows and podcasts, to develop all kinds of programs, also through the art section, the artists are exposed to how they are generating this step by step of a project, the same happens with the music category because it is where artists broadcast live their songs and fulfill requests or answer questions.

Beyond the type of content you choose, you can use a system of tags to filter and specialize the search, these are words in gray that are found under the direct, if you click on these, the website itself is responsible for reordering the streamings that are related to this tag.

Another way to search on this platform, is manually on the search engine, you also need to pay attention to the tags that are trending at the moment, for each type of category you will find two divisions, between video and clip, these provide deferred content, such as live recordings of other previous dates.

This means that when you miss some kind of stream you have the opportunity to relive it, but the distinction about these sections is that "videos" is about grouping together full broadcasts, which can last up to more than two hours, whereas clips are short fragments that are presented as the best moments and are sometimes created by fans.

In Twitch there is a lot to find, since it is a platform that can be used for different purposes, content creators have the opportunity to innovate, which is why channels have emerged that are closely related to the explanation and discussion of politics.

- **What you can do while enjoying a live performance**

Once you select a channel you like, you can click on "follow", this is a symbol described as a purple heart, thereby attaching it to your list, so that you receive notifications, such as a notice that Twitch issues about the next time the channel goes live.

If at any time you want to stop receiving notifications, you just have to deactivate the bell, or if you regret following a channel and want to stop following it, just click on the heart again, in case you know a user who might like the channel, you can just click on the up arrow icon.

Above the tray is the option to recommend a channel, thus alternatives arise to share the URL to post it on social networks or any other media, likewise when a content breaks the rules of the platform such as racist comments, sexual content and others, you can denounce the creator.

On the right side you can see the chat options, you must follow the channel in advance, then click on "send a message", so you can write and send whatever you want, as long as you do not violate any rules, in this mode you can use emojis by clicking on the face.

These options cause that you can visualize the most used emojis, in the same way you can customize the emojis of this chat, or any other type of expression, but when they have padlocks it means that you must follow and subscribe to the channel to use it, in case the chat bothers you too much you can click on the arrow to minimize it.

In the course of the chat you may come across someone you like, you can follow them by clicking on their name, you can click on the two options, add friend or whisper, it is normal to first select whisper so that you have the opportunity to send a message and introduce yourself so that you can add each other.

You can also click on the little people icon above the chat, in this way you will invoke a list of users so that you will have the contact you are interested in.

The valuable content offered in Twitch strea-mings.

To think about the kind of value you can create and offer on Twitch, it is simple when you browse through the whole platform to get an idea about what is offered, also as long as you understand the way this platform is developed or its way of being, it will be easier to be part of this kind of environment.

Following the idea that many people gather to enjoy streaming helps you build content that meets those expectations, especially when different factors are present on this kind of platform, usually the channels that receive more attention are those that expose demos or advance versions of the most followed games.

In the case of Call of Duty fans, they may be interested in streamers that broadcast some delivery or trick on this subject, likewise when you watch some gameplays that works as a help to address any questions about a game, but when you doubt that this is your forte, it is best to bet on another route.

The essential thing is that you know completely about the subject you expect to deal with, that is why it is a wide dedication, because the intention is that your account is a means for you to discover more details about that delivery, without thinking about money or fame in the same way it needs to be a delivery with which you have fun.

It is not advisable to start with a heavy investment, but to try with valuable options that help you to have a good start to increase the level until you create a community that follows you, the important thing is to make the decision to prepare yourself and be creative on that topic to show the best of it.

In order not to be redundant, you cannot lose sight of the establishment of a creative theme, where your personality is also a point of attraction, since the content is not only chosen by the title but by what the streamer transmits, because the intention is that the user can have a good time and above all that he/she can interact.

Becoming successful on Twitch is possible when you appeal to charisma, it is a way to play with personality to broadcast the best possible presentation, this is why it is mentioned that it is a set of factors to become a famous online streamer.

Learn about Prime gaming payment or channel subscriptions

As you start to like the Twitch platform more, you're going to want to make a paid subscription, although they may arise about whether it turns out to be a profitable investment or not, so you should know that the main subscription that you can run out of is called as Twitch Gaming, but it was originally called Twitch Prime.

This type of payment provides different advantages, but it does not mean that the free version does not provide benefits, because when you like a channel you can enjoy it without having to pay the creator, while the paid mode refers to a matter of exclusivity that you do not get by other means.

The Prime mode is booming, especially because the payment is included on Amazon Prime since 2014 that this company bought the platform, this means that if you have Amazon Prime you can count on Prime Gaming, this type of subscription alone has a cost of 4 euros per month.

That kind of offer is ideal for everything it provides, but mostly it's more cost-effective to buy Amazon Prime to have that extra Twitch bonus, on the other hand, there are the individual subscription offerings, the important thing is that beforehand you know that on each channel you're going to find a wide offering.

Likewise, each channel can maintain a monthly subscription offering, so you can pay to get more benefits, each of these subscriptions are responsible for sharing or offering a set of innovations on the channel and content, which highlights the fact that no ads appear during broadcasts.

The exclusive chat is an option that is not available to everyone, the same happens with the video catalog that is intended only for this type of subscribers, the other benefits are due to a design issue, in addition to being unlocked different emojis that can be customized.

The paid registration of a channel is carried out as a demonstration of liking for the creation of content that is made, especially when you are looking to issue an economic support to continue producing these videos, that is what motivates users to pay, that is more for admiration than for any choice of utility.

The level of security offered by Twitch

By placing twitch as one of the favorite platforms and adding them to your browser, you can carry out the profile settings, but before any aesthetic changes, it is best that you can familiarize yourself with the security and privacy section, because it is a platform where some hackers can emerge.

Prevention within any platform is never too much, so a first step you can take is to create a long password, this can be formed by uppercase, lowercase, numbers and a punctuation mark, this generates discomfort for many, but it is the best guarantee that you are not an easy target for hacking.

On the other hand, you can opt for the two-step authentication configuration, this works as a layer of protection at the beginning before logging into the account, that way when someone tries to access your account they won't be able to, as they even issue a code to change the password.

Beyond the hacks, a constant questioning arises through the type of content that may arise for children or minors, but you should know that Twitch is not a platform created or designed for the purpose of hosting minors, although it has a serious policy of moderating content so that it is not violent or offensive.

But in some content may leak something that is inappropriate for children, also most of the games discussed are of the violent category, above the content there is also the risk that arises about the chats, as they would have access to chat with strangers and these can send some private message.

In this type of situations the platform has options to help block both users and channels, but the reality is that it is a platform that is not recommended for children under 13 years old, so they should not use it, in case they have favorite gamers it is best to watch it on YouTube through their excerpts.

The various themes on Twitch

Every video game lover is fully aware of what Twitch offers, but in the same way all kinds of content have emerged that are acclaimed by the community that in turn prefers streaming content, this has been increasing year after year, especially with the events that are held every year.

More people in the world enter Twitch for different reasons, for this reason it is a space to enter and have an account, because if you are a lover of video broadcasts this is an opportunity to show your talent, especially to take advantage of the excessive growth that this platform is having.

Twitch's global community is available to any user, which is why it is classified as a social network, reaching the same level as Facebook, Instagram and even YouTube, and its global quality is due to Amazon's push for every player to be able to live stream for users who can interact.

Learn the steps to create a Twitch account

To create a Twitch account you only have to follow a few simple steps, through which you will be able to take full advantage of the features of this platform, the steps are as follows:

1. Log on to https://www.twitch.tv/.

2. Click on the corner where it indicates the "Register" option.
3. Complete the requested fields with your personal data, this involves establishing your username, password and date of birth.
4. Choose well the e-mail as a means of contact.
5. You can take advantage of connecting the platform with Facebook, so you can start with Facebook.

Once you carry out this brief process, you can have a functional account to carry out the broadcasts and gain popularity over time, using each of the options that the platform has.

How Twitch works

Creating a Twitch account and making its alternatives work is simple, but the first steps you should take seriously is to fully understand how this type of platform works, so that the content you present will be able to exceed any expectations.

• Explore Twitch

This option allows you as a new user to get to know everything you can find on this platform, just click on the explore button to have access to a wide list of categories, thus presenting the available contents that you can start viewing.

On the cover of each title you can see how many people are online, this allows you to click on the cover of the game to see who is streaming on that topic, you can also change in the menu where the "Showing" option is to go from categories to live channels sorted by the number of visitors.

- **The channels you follow**

This is a list of the channels to which you are subscribed, where you can have access to the users that appear "Offline" if they are not online, or those that are broadcasting at that moment, in case they are online at that moment, it means that they are active.

- **Featured channels**

They are Twitch channels that you are invited to follow because they are the most popular within that community, it's like a kind of suggestion on the subject matter you follow, so that you select the most prominent accounts in that environment.

- **Gameplay, swag and other Twitch Prime details**

This type of offering corresponds with weekly rewards, so you can get donations and other monetization that Twitch Prime has.

- **Notifications**

They can be activated through the little bell icon, this is a way through which you can receive notifications about any change that is generated on the platform, these changes can be new subscribers, achievements, and other types of messages about the channels you are following, or some other news of this type.

- **Get bits**

Bits are used as a reward system that can be purchased to be shared or used with favorite creators, this type of reward system is an incentive on an economic level.

- **Profile tools and functions**

Here you can find all the features, tools, configurations and other settings about the control panel to manage your Twitch account.

Twitch Prime and all it stands for

The operation of Twitch Prime translates into a Premium version of this platform, this version helps you get a whole series of gifts that are unlocked with each progress, in addition to granting and designing exclusive content, but the best thing is the enjoyment of the content without any advertising.

Since Twitch is owned by Amazon, it is offered through the acquisition of Amazon Prime or Prime Video accounts with Twitch Prime content, this happens automatically.

Learn how to stream on Twitch

It is a broadcast like the one that takes place on YouTube or Facebook Live, it can also be carried out through OBS, this is simple and you only have to follow a configuration that at first glance may seem complex, but if you follow these steps you can carry out the transmission:

1. Enter OBS Studio, it must be previously downloaded.
2. Click on File, then on configuration until you click on "Emission".
3. The next thing to select is the type of broadcast, you must click on; retransmission service.
4. In the service section, click on "Twitch".
5. Through the server, you can enter the "Automatic" option.
6. Where it says broadcast key you must paste the Twitch channel's broadcast key.

To find the broadcast key, you just need to log in Twitch account, then in the corner where your user name appears you need to click, the next thing is to enter the control panel, and enter the settings to click on "channel", then you can select to show the main broadcast key.

It is important that you read the notice issued by the platform, so that you agree with all the conditions and click on "understood", then you only have to copy it to use it in OBS.

Twitch control panel features

The Twitch control panel is one of the important points to consider, since this streamer platform has several preferences when broadcasting, for this reason it has a wide configuration service, you just have to pay attention to each option to get the best out of the channel, these options are useful.

By means of some particular selection you can manage to earn money by means of Twitch, this adds more relevance to these steps, so you should discover the following basic settings:

1. **Live**

The information about the broadcast is located on this section, thanks to these options you can find the title of the broadcast, the notifications about what happens during the live broadcast, the category to which the content belongs, up to the tags and the language.

2. Title

You have 140 characters to enter a title to the broadcast, so you can try to make it eye-catching to gain users, that is the way to attract a lot of people, so when someone comes across your transmission will not cause hesitation in entering to see the content.

3. Live broadcast notifications

It is a type of message that appears to followers when you are broadcasting live, but it is better to take this opportunity to emerge with creativity by writing a call to action that can bring results, to achieve this you can create a text of 140 characters for this purpose.

4. Category

To choose the type of category you should only focus on the type of content you are going to publish, this detail deserves importance because if you select another category that is not related to the topic, you will not get the right viewers, since they will not find your content because they will be in the wrong place.

5. **Tags**

Tags represent a crucial point, but these are underestimated by most users on Twitch, when in fact they can achieve furt- her with your account by devoting the attention they deserve, these are used to describe the broadcast or indirection, above the category.

Most viewers use them to find broadcasts that are of interest to them, as they work as a kind of filter to rule out the content you are looking for from a wide catalog, so when searching for specific tags and exploring recommendations, they are the avenues through which a large number of users reach the channel.

Twitch is in charge of managing the issue of tags, because it seeks to offer a selection that is available, but you have the opportunity to customize and add some, following the com- ments you receive and according to the type of content you are transmitting.

Ideally, the tags should follow the same aspirations of the community, so you can include even a specific type of tag, to choose the appropriate one you can follow some suggestions or research the tags available on the subject that has domain in the retransmissions you make.

Tags are found next to the thumbnail or excerpt of the video, meaning that it must be compatible with the title of the video as well as the category, that way you will get the attention you are looking for, in the case of directory pages this is a space where viewers can use tags to filter category directories.

Based on what users are looking for, they can be achieved with the tags you place, i.e. if a user only places art, and you want to draw the attention of people who have that preference, certainly the tag should be composed of that word, although you can use custom recommendations as a system where tags are estimated.

When recommending new transmissions according to the type of viewing history you have, you should follow or use the tag that is most repeated within the community you want to reach, i.e. that makes you more eligible to their preferences, the same happens with the tags that are most searched.

The inclusion of tags has a lot to do with live broadcasts, as they are included above the broadcast information section, this is done through the live control panel, this can be done by channel owners as well as editors.

Some tags are added automatically along with the language, in case you want to change the language you must enter the live broadcast in the Live Control Panel, the installation of the tags must be updated just as it happens with the titles, since their function is to describe the current broadcast when the channel broadcasts a live broadcast.

When you are broadcasting live via a third-party broadcasting software, it is essential that you do not forget to incorporate the corresponding tags via the live control panel, or ask a channel editor to take care of this function.

The design of the tags seeks to help the viewer to find the ideal content, according to their interests they can find just what they want, and these may not be linked to that category or topic in particular, this allows you to gain freedom at the time of establishing a tag to describe the transmission.

This means that you can transmit trending content without the need for the video to be part of that category, the important thing is that you dedicate time and effort to the description of the transmission, always with an objective vision so that the content can be recommended without problems and directed towards the viewers that suit you.

In the case of publishing games or content that is competitive, you should not add a tag that says "exciting", otherwise the content will not appear above the section or the list of featured videos.

6. Language

The language that appears in most of the options, goes hand in hand with the language you use for your broadcast, you can also select the one that is appropriate for your nationality, and when you determine a specific language, you can generate the access to the broadcast of that specific language.

When you set the language appropriately, you get the help for the account to be found effectively and without wasting so much time, so it is a detail that should not be underestimated.

7. Extensions

The extensions correspond to different applications or plugins that are installed to make adjustments to the broadcasts, so that the channel can receive a higher level of value, because there is a wide variety of them to meet your objectives, so you can find the one that can be adapted to your needs.

8. **Achievements**

A platform like Twitch also has an incentive such as some achievements, so once you manage to complete certain steps, you will have the possibility to unlock some features that the platform has, or you can simply use it as a distraction, the important thing is that you motivate yourself as a streamer to be the best.

9. **Events**

The events are those that work along the same lines as those organized by Facebook, for which a photo is usually published with the title, description of the event, start and end date, the language in which it will be held, even the category, these events are generally interesting and an opportunity at the same time, to make a launch.

10. **Activity**

The activity is a factor where all the functions or steps carried out are summarized, that is to say that what you do on Twitch will be reflected on this section, it is based on a history of the account so that you can take into account the modifications, retransmissions and any other type of activity as its name indicates.

11. Transmission tools

This set of tools are programs that can be used to create and set up your live broadcasts, there are all kinds you can imagine, from paid to free, it is common to use OBS, to make the most of its features you must familiarize yourself with what it offers.

A key step is to obtain the most recent version of OBS, where you can find sections for testing, as well as the fonts to be used during the recording, so these steps are recommended to be done in advance, that way you will have everything covered at the time of recording.

There is also the option of the browser show so that you will be able to include some kind of screenshot, as well as verify the audio input that the broadcast will have, all these are preparation details to illustrate the type of video or content that you are going to create.

The software aims to project the same as you are watching behind the screen, as well as help manage the use of hardware such as the microphone, the image of the broadcast you can decrease and expand as it is better for the video, another curious function is to capture the audio and game server.

When you start the game, this free program is responsible for capturing all kinds of details, in turn you can recognize the game to apply the settings that are most appropriate, the management of the webcam is useful when it comes to making broadcasts, this is a way to have full control of the recording.

Scenes can be added at the time of including the video, and you can include images to create a presentation with transitions, this is one of the most common utilities that had received this type of program, which allows you to customize the broadcast in the way and style you want, without forgetting the inclusion of text that can be carried out.

12. Analysis

It is defined as a section to find data about the broadcasts, from sociodemographic points of viewers, as well as the hours of reproduction, among other details, so you can make decisions about your content, this helps you take seriously your progress as a streamer.

To get to monetize within this platform you can not fail to reinforce these aspects, it also helps to design a strategy thanks to the analysis of this type of data, it is a measure to be able to improve.

13. Videos

It is a mode or a section to publish your own videos that have been edited, this makes it easy to expose them as a fake live, so you can organize the entire section in collections, so that you form clips of videos that belong to other streamers, i.e. they are saved and can be seen again at another time.

Additional channel configurations

Through the settings found in the control panel, you can access one of the most important parts of presenting yourself as a successful streamer, so you should recognize the following points:

- **Channel**

In this section you can find the transmission key that you must use to start with OBS, this is reiterated because many times you lose track of the location of this key, through this section you can select if you want to save the previous broadcasts, you have a maximum period of 14 days to keep it as a normal user.

In case you are a Prime, partner or turbo user, you have 60 days to have the video saved, also within the options you can set whether it is adult content, which does not mean that it is pornography, but that violence ads or other measures are broadcasted before the transmission begins.

On the other hand you can choose the optimization preference, this helps you that the video quality can go hand in hand with the broadcast, i.e. in case you have little power in the pc, it may be complex to run two tasks, such as the game and the OBS, you can select the "low latency" measure.

On the other hand, when you have a great team that can support you, you can continue broadcasting without limitations, another point that you must take care of is the permissions, since you have the power to choose if other people can broadcast the content of your channel.

An aesthetic aspect that provides better presence is to create a banner that can appear when the channel is deactivated, that way followers can enter and watch a previous video, without the need for that annoying black image that remains on the screen, because the more authentic you are, the more users you will attract.

The features make it easy to manage permissions on the community, where you can grant and designate an editor to the extent that he/she has the same functions as the channel owner, the same goes for the inclusion of a moderator who is in charge of managing a friendly chat environment.

On the other hand, there are the VIP users that are described as outstanding on the community, from the same you can find the settings on the moderation so that everyone who wants can be in contact with you, participation in the chat is an aspect that you should not neglect, you can also have an email verifier.

Ways to gain followers on Twitch

Once you have your channel set up, know each function and configuration, the next step is to create a channel that is eye-catching, so that your content will be one of the most visited, using everything OBS has to offer to the fullest, in addition to the fact that you must have previously identified the topic you are going to deal with on the transmission.

Starting to strim is simple when you cover these basic aspects, the essential thing is that you take into account the variety of channels as a motivation not as something discouraging, because you can get followers as long as you propose it as a goal, since the level of traffic that is on this platform is an opportunity.

As long as you have something unique to offer through your channel, you can exploit to the maximum the possibilities to grow that will be presented to you, for this you can use and put into practice some tips to become a great streamer such as the following actions:

1. Define what type of streamer you are

What you want to be in the middle of Twitch is a basic point to grow on this platform, since you need to think first of all if it is a game, then if you are going to play all the modes or only the premieres, consequently, you must define the type of console you are going to use, in addition to the style to choose either retro or new.

Once you can answer these basic and important questions, you can make decisions to grow on that medium or topic, to the point of monetizing with your account, this is a really fundamental point for your future on this platform.

2. Build a value strategy

It is vital that when you enter Twitch, you can dedicate yourself to broadcasting because you are passionate about it, but not because you are only looking to gain fame, because this is perceived by users, you must spread empathy and liking for this content, if you do not comply with this you can be crushed by the competition that uses much more charisma.

The formation of a strategy does not imply taking it so seriously to the point of losing naturalness, since it is then noticed live that you follow an inflexible script, the most valuable thing is that you have fun with what you transmit, that way you will get more users to see you to the point of gaining more users in your favor.

3. Identify what's best about your offering

Every community is formed when it is achieved with a value proposition, so you must know yourself to promote your channel, if you are an expert on the subject and seek to share with followers all your tricks, you are forming a profile that will provide each person, but this must be combined with your personality.

The way you explain a broadcast matters a lot, that's an added value that can be defined in the way you teach others, you must take the time to learn the best way to achieve it, that's why it can be a redundant topic on Twitch, but it is presented by more than 1000 ways to explain it.

The best thing you can select is what suits you best, think about or prioritize the type of personality you possess, that way you can find the answers about what you want to do, although the point of it all is to create a nice moment for people to see you, that flashy side is what you can't lose.

4. **Keep the constancy**

To be a professional streamer you must implement consistency, this is necessary for everything you propose, so it is a great idea to set times for recording, to create the habit of allocating those days for that activity, you should also study the time most frequented by users, this helps you gain traffic during transmissions.

When you broadcast content on a regular basis, you will get users to remember you, for this you must also think about the needs of users, that is, when you can have access to the highest concentration of that community, it is essential that you have a fixed measure of content creation so that in turn it is easy to promote it.

5. **Conduct sweepstakes or reward your community**

Nothing excites a community of followers more than gifts, so a good way to gain people's appreciation is through this channel, so organizing a contest and offering gifts is a good motivation for them to approach the channel, the most competitive is a sweepstakes because it helps you gain traffic.

6. Creates and plans strategies on other social networks

Twitch is recognized as a social network itself, but you can use traffic from other social networks to make yourself known, i.e. you can implement a Social Media plan, this should be adjusted to the theme of the channel, as well as a way to share valuable content, causing your followers are encouraged to enter Twitch to your channel.

You can't forget to ask them to follow you through other social networks, this works as a springboard to grow on this platform, the main requirement is that you establish relationships with users and stay active sharing content, while still making yourself known so that you attract attention.

Conversation with users is a good way to share content, also with other streamers you can help each other as an exchange of promotion, that way you both become known using each other's community.

7. **Participate in events and networking**

Events on the topic you are dedicated to on Twitch are a bri-lliant springboard, that way you can go far using a local com-munity, to gain virtual support, plus you need to be recog-nized in the medium or at least get involved with an activity in that environment that can draw the attention of people or users.

Events are gaining more and more strength, especially when it comes to video games, you can create virtual activities, such as competing with other streamers, so that the popula-rity of all merge into a transmission that can move a lot of traffic that is beneficial to all.

In broadcasting you can become an expert as long as you take each step seriously, plus you have the option to network with other streamers to use that support to your advantage, as well as to present attractive content for that sector, as there is nothing more exciting than a good event.

8. **Learn and develop graphic design actions**

Your channel can be shaped as best suits the type of content you present, think of it as decorating a room and in that way you will create a channel that is competitive, as long as it emits a perfect image you will make the design speak for you, it will be a presentation itself.

If designing is not your thing and you do not want to make big investments on this topic, you can use some simple tools that can help you, these are totally online and with an intuitive operation so that you are able to achieve to present a great design, among the options Canva stands out.

There are many ways to make followers fall in love through design, the important thing is that you can go further, i.e. to look for a perfect image for the theme, because that helps to make the customization and that users can recognize you, so you can seek support to have an intro video before issuing a streaming.

9. **Relay through other social media channels**

Beyond the fact that Twitch is one of the number one broadcasting platforms, you can also use other social media to get the word out about your content, you can use recaps, excerpts, funny bits and more to draw attention to other social video networks.

You can try broadcasting your content through Facebook Live or even on YouTube, the important thing is that it is a varied proposal, that way you can diversify your followers and take the attraction you generate from one platform to another, it may be something that requires dedication, but it is worth it to grow and become known.

10. Researches and implements Neuromarketing

As an expert it is common that you want to cause more and more impact with your content, for this reason the study of neuromarketing is very useful to convey emotion and above all to win the affection of viewers, the minds of your users can be dominated as long as you take care to cause attraction.

11. Do not use the phrase "follow me and I will follow you".

This type of desperate methodology to get followers only leaves you as a desperate account, it only works or is more appropriate when you use it when starting out in this medium, and you can apply this text on forums, but with the objective that it reaches people who are in the same situation as you, in terms of progress.

The "follow me and I'll follow you" proposition can cause embarrassment, especially when it comes to scaling on a platform where you should be interested in the type of content you present or the subject matter, this is not a bad strategy, but you should not get used to this.

Find out how to make money on Twitch

Being a streamer generates many benefits, among these is the opportunity to generate income, this is a reality when you have an acceptable performance, ie the content must be good for your channel to monetize the way you expect, to achieve this task you can follow some tips.

A key step to generating money is to learn as much as you can about Twitch, this also includes keeping up with reading every new thing that is added to this platform, next is to take on your role as a streamer as professionally as you can, but without getting to the point of obsessing about making money.

The process of monetizing on Twitch is a fact that needs patience, as it does not happen overnight, but you can keep in mind that Amazon has an affiliate program and this same happens with Twitch, in this case the platform itself is responsible for inviting you to be one, but you must meet some requirements such as the following:

- Meet a retransmission level of 500 minutes in the last 30 days.
- To have carried out retransmission during the last 7 days, about 30 days.
- Have an average of 3 viewers at the same time in the last 30 days.
- Have at least 50 followers.
- Maintain a two-step authenticated account.

An additional way to generate money is through the donation system, this is based on activating a banner that allows followers to be able to make financial donations as a contribution to the channel, i.e. it is based on a show of support for the content.

Additionally you can use another type of affiliate system, for this you must share some links that allow you to earn commission when someone buys through the link, this follows the same dynamic that develops in the Amazon affiliate system or as happens with other video game stores as is the case of G2A.

Twitch develops a Bit system, this allows you to get a penny every time someone uses a Bit to send a cheers on the channel.

The Twitchcon celebration

The Twitchcon celebration is known as an event that is held annually, it is an offering of the best that the platform has to offer, this celebration takes place over an entire weekend, to organize and celebrate activities, streams, tournaments and much more, that is a compilation for the true fans.

The announcement of this event has a lot to do with the development of a large number of activities, thereby raising the level of traffic that it is able to generate by itself as a platform, so it is a topic to which to devote importance because your participation can lead you to gain followers.

Twitch offering over video games

This point is relevant for those who believe that only Twitch is about video games, because the categories within the platform extend, one of which is taking more popularity is IRL, it is known as a space for channels dedicated to Talk Shows and also podcast.

Everything related to music and performing arts receives a special treatment, in addition, science and technology topics have a good reception on this platform, and users dealing with role-playing games, or the explanation of a craft such as working with paint, that kind of vision has great scalability on this medium.

Events can also be reported through this platform, along with the inclusion of sports and fitness, as well as people cooking and even eating live to taste a dish, which is also causing interest among the user community.

In the middle of IRL one of the channels that is gaining more place is Just Chatting, where users sit down and use the webcam to talk about some weird incidence that happens, as long as the platform's policy issues are safeguarded, because privacy cannot be broken through Twitch.

This type of content creation shines because it is so interesting, by itself is a theme that invites to participate constantly, these have been seconded to the same level of video game championships, so it is a way that is established to prevail and more people are delighted by this way.

Earning a living through these topics is an alternative that is gaining strength, the essential thing is that viewers enjoy what they are watching, that kind of motivation is what you must awaken so that the rising trends gain their own space, especially with generation Z or V, which are the most predominant online.

The Twitch experience can be diversified, as long as you find a way to broadcast under an original style, this is what makes it possible that a greater number of users stick to the content you broadcast, this goes hand in hand with the preferences that arise from digital marketing, where creativity fits on the content.

What you need to know to get started on Twitch

One of the previous considerations to start on Twitch and gain popularity, is to think from the view of the viewers, to find what millions of people like and are passionate about, that way you can match their tastes, this website dedicated to live streaming is emerging as one of the largest platforms.

When it comes to this purpose, it is presented as an opportunity or a means to reach more than 15 million viewers, so it becomes a space to demonstrate that professional talent to reach more people, presenting video game games, interviews, sessions and broadcasting all kinds of content.

Becoming famous is an option under all the alternatives that this platform has, so you must start by being a real streamer and arouse sympathy, in addition to meeting the hardware requirements necessary to meet the expectations of viewers, but also to develop the subject matter without obvious flaws.

- **Requirements to broadcast on your Twitch channel**

A basic step that you must exhaust is to show the content in the best way to the viewers, for this it is vital to cover certain basic measures so that your digital proposal is interesting and attractive at the same time, but it is important that you can count on a good PC or a game console that are suitable for the theme you want to develop.

By having this, you can dedicate yourself to have a software to carry out the quality streaming you are looking to provide, this also includes the use of microphone so you have a higher level of audio clarity, it is usually best to invest in headphones that incorporate the microphone because it represents greater comfort.

In the same way the camera plays an important role, as it is the one that makes up the content so that fans can enjoy it, it is important that you know just how to broadcast from the PC, for this you can view some tutorials that teach you the previous steps, to master the recording from Xbox One, PS4, Nintendo Switch and others.

The guides on this type of configuration are of great help for you to be able to achieve quality results, as well as to integrate more elements such as screenshots, clips, and to implement some tips that prioritize the aesthetic level.

- **Recommended devices for streamings**

The development of the streamings requires the inclusion of suitable equipment, although in some topics there are exceptions that cause that the transmission from a computer is not so complicated or expensive, in the same way being a streamer involves continuous investment so you can progress and be better and better.

In the case of the Twitch platform itself, it recommends covering the requirements of having an Intel Core i5-4670 processor or one that is equivalent to AMD, the corresponding RAM memory must be 8 GB, and the operating system must be Windows 7 or higher, in the same way it can be done from a Mac.

For the transmission of PC games, you must have a graphics card that has enough power or power, the essential is that they support the execution of both programs, these must be able to accept to work with a DirectX 10 and higher, in the case of the Internet, you must use a connection that is fast and stable.

These measures are recommended and the best for you to have fluidity in the creation of content, regarding the internet you should incorporate an upload speed of 3 MB per second, this is feasible for most internet connections, if you wonder about broadcasting from a mobile or a computer, the latter is always recommended.

Using the desktop of a computer you can start and carry out the broadcast, because broadcasting content from a computer that is portable is a reality, as long as it can meet the basic specifications to take care of the quality, in the case of using a mobile device you must ensure that it exceeds the expectations of users.

The requirements of the central system that Twitch has are very accessible, both for transmission or streaming, as well as for the reproduction of games that have a high graphic level, although it is true that they demand a considerable load on the PC does not saturate it completely.

For this reason some streamers who have a great popularity online use two PCs to alleviate and distribute the load, because one is used to load the games and another for the transmission, this can be complex to install or master at the beginning, but you can use programs like CyberPower that facilitates the management of two PCs in the same tower.

- **Key details in the creation of the Twitch account**

Customized joining through Twitch can be developed through https://www.twitch.tv, so you can join the platform so that you can carry out the broadcast, where you must select an avatar, banner and description, so you can create a presentation so that you are attractive to users.

At the same time you must incorporate the configuration of archiving the broadcasts, so you have access to them temporarily, this causes that you can see it later, through the configuration option, then in channel and videos you will find the archive broadcasts.

- **The software you need for streaming on Twitch**

A key tool or part to perform the streaming on Twitch is the transmission software, that way you will share the content with users, the most used programs to fulfill this purpose is the Open Broadcasting Software (OBS), which is completely free.

On the other hand, there is the XSplit software, this allows or has an easy to use interface because its options are intuitive, but its functions are offered through a paid subscription to offer exclusivity, beyond the selection of the software, you must implement a configuration on the transmission.

In the middle of the transmission and its settings, it is vital to select the sources with which you want to perform the streaming, this means choosing the type of computer monitor, the original source of the game or the webcam, likewise it is vital to establish or set the way in which the elements will appear to the viewer.

The choice of the skin or overlay is important because it is the text that appears as a viewer subscribes to the channel, the same goes for the incorporation of details about the chat, the formation of the donation feed to monetize the channel if you meet the conditions described.

Finally, one of the settings that you must make is to synchronize your Twitch account, so that you will be able to broadcast the live streams you want, taking the necessary precautions and care.

- **Incorporation of camera and microphone**

If you do not have a webcam, and the theme of the channel is based on you having contact with the community, you should choose a device that allows you to show your face, for this the selection of Logitech HD Pro C920 is one of the best selections you can make, because it offers a quality capture based on 1080p.

This means that it is a wide field of view, so you can carry out the recording, the Logitech C922 model has the same 1080p quality, but has an automatic background removal, this means that you can appear in the game without having to place a green screen.

On the other hand, there is also the function of the Razer Kiyo, this has similar qualities to provide the sharpness to cancel the light that is incorporated so that your face can be distinguished without any problem, although at a technical level you can use headphones for streaming, it is best to invest in a microphone.

The more specialized equipment you use, the better results you can get, and the microphone causes the audience to hear you clearly, one of the most purchased for this purpose is Blue Yeti that can be used via USB connection, it also provides high quality audio and a way to collect noise that fits.

If you do not have much budget to start streaming in this way, you can scale up or consider other more economical devices, such as the purchase of Samson Go Mic, for its portable qualities and the purchase of Razer Seiren, these options are useful to present a professional image of you.

Streaming on Twitch via video game consoles

In the case of having an Xbox One or PS4 console, you have the possibility to broadcast from the console itself, without the need to use another type of device or extra software, through Xbor One you only have to download the Twitch application, you can get it for free.

In the case of wanting to transmit from PS4 you only have to scroll to the menu to share from the system itself, although through Xbox you can also take advantage of this type of option to connect directly with the Twitch platform, in addition to the free application that has the Microsoft Store.

Similarly, in both cases it is easy to comply with these steps, although the limitation of using a console to backcast is that you can not make adjustments or customization as you can do from a PC, but it is still an effective alternative to be part of the streaming world.

When you want to stream via Nintendo Switch or a similar console, you can gain control over the stream via a capture card, which you can register in the console game on your PC, so you can have better managed content with your own personality stamp.

That last option of retransmission through the capture card is a popular solution within this medium, usually the one that is frequently used is the Elgato Game Capture HD, which allows you to record 1080p videos that are carried out from an Xbox One, 360 and also on PS4, PS3 and Wii U.

Regardless of the type of console, or the type of system with HDMI output, the capture card works ideally, you can add the component adapters that allow you to realize a retro-style broadcast, to cover some smooth or smooth 60 frames per second recordings, you can raise the level up to the point of HD60.

Broadcasting on Twitch using a PC

If you are passionate about video games mostly, you can enter Twitch to transmit the games, the same happens when you want to create some kind of program, because it is a pioneer platform in the subject of transmissions, for that reason it hosts up to 140 million monthly viewers in a unique way.

The type of retransmission that attracts the most attention is Fortnite, PlayerUknowns's, World of Warcraft and the other shows held at the rate of art and cooking categories, where sports content also gains space, plus anyone can create original content to take advantage of Twitch's broadcasting options.

In addition to the usual PS4 and Xbox One gaming capabilities, they also have streaming capabilities, in case you want to do it from a PC you just need to have hardware that can meet the demands of this streaming activity, in addition to implementing a streaming software to use your Twitch account.

Sharing your content on Twitch with the world is simple, because you only have to register to start enjoying its live operation, it is an ideal platform for anyone, and you only have to set up the following configurations to start broadcasting:

1. Install the retransmission application on the PC, for this you can incorporate different solutions such as the use of Open Broadcaster Software (OBS), this is available for

Windows, Mac and Linux, likewise XSplit is designed for Windows.

OBS is free to use, thanks to the fact that it is an open source medium, but it needs to cover some additional configurations, while XSplit has intuitive options, although its options depend on a paid subscription to have access to its features.

2. Log in to Twitch and sign in.
3. Select the Control Panel from the drop-down menu, so that you can make the desired settings at the top right of the screen.
4. Find and click on the type of game you wish to play through the "Play" tab.
5. Access the title so that you can effectively carry out the retransmission.

If you wish to use OBS, you must also carry out a configuration on the retransmission, based on these steps:

1. Click on the right button that has OBS, and choose the way to run as administrator, that is vital to use Game Capture.
2. Choose the transmission configuration via the configuration menu.

3. Select Twitch as a streaming service, then you can click on Optimize at the bottom left of the menu.
4. Return to the Twitch panel and select Strem Key, then follow the instructions to receive the unique broadcast code.
5. Copy and paste this code into the Stream Key box above the configuration menu and click "Ok".

The next thing to do is to set the scene for you to go live, after these actions:

1. Through the OBS central interface, you can right-click to enter the "Sources" box to add the game capture.
2. Select the type of game you are using, thanks to the menu that pops up to click on accept.
3. Right click again on the "Fonts" box, you can then incorporate any additional fonts, this allows you to enter images and text to help facilitate the layout, you can use Monitor Capture to display what you want on the screen, or select Video Capture to launch the webcam.
4. Enter the stream preview to modify the scene, this is applied to fit completely to the design you have in mind, i.e. you may be using a stream of the game, but you want to present a highlight or your explanation, this can be added in a corner of the stream.

5. Click to start the transmission through the OBS control panel, that way you will be completely live.

When using XSplit, you can configure the streaming by following the steps below:

1. Open and enter the XSplit.
2. Select the "Broadcast" option to add the channel to Twitch in the near future.
3. Authorize and enter your Twitch username and password.
4. Finally you must click on finish, so that XSplit will automatically set the most appropriate resolution.
5. Configure the transmission properties and click OK.

Set the scene for you to go live, by following these steps:

1. Go to the Screen Sources section at the bottom left of the XSplit interface and click on "Add".
2. Go to the game capture, to select the game you are going to implement.
3. Add an additional source, such as images, or webcam streaming.
4. Drag the source to your liking, this means that when you want to present in the feed the game capture, as a welcome highlight, you can do it by means of a box in the corner that exposes the webcam.

5. Then you can select Broadcast, then Twitch, and that way you will be live.

How to stream on Twitch through Xbox One

If you have an Xbox One, and you want to become a popular streamer, you can start streaming from this console itself, this is a plus point to show that you are good, in games of the size or caliber of Fortnite, this can be done with a few small previous adjustments.

You just need to get the platform up and running for you to use Twitch, thanks to these steps:

- Download and use the free Twitch app available through the Xbox Store.
- Log in, for this you must have an active registration in Twitch, so you can start broadcasting from the application itself.
  - Enter https://twitch.tv/activate through a browser or a PC, Tablet and also a cell phone, you only need to enter a code that appears on the screen.
- Open the game you wish to stream via the Xbox One.
- Press twice on the home button, so you can enter the menu and at the bottom you can choose Twitch, so if you

have Kinect or microphone connected to the console, you can enter Twitch just by mentioning "Cortana, broadcast", or by "Cortana, open Twitch", when the application is open you must click on broadcast.

- Assign a name to the transmission, so you can use the configuration menu before starting, this is so you can adjust the operation of microphone, Kinect, chat and others, so you can choose the level of quality that has the transmission.

- Log in to start the stream and activate it, this can be seen closely in the Twitch chat to modify the settings via the right side of the screen, you can also hide the Twitch sidebar by double tapping the home button and selecting the "Unpin" option, or by saying "Cortana, unpin".

In this way you will be live in a short period of time, also in Google Play you can find a free and downloadable application, it has a lot of utilities to configure the broadcast in real time, it also works to check how the transmission is going to be.

The incorporation of the title of the broadcast is possible through this tool, and it facilitates everything when sharing the link to see the live stream on other social networks, you can search for other broadcasts, in addition to other powers.

Learn how to stream on Twitch through PS4

To share the games in the world you can use the PS4, as it has Twitch streaming compatibility, as you can start directly from the console, being of ample use in case you are looking to start with Resident Evil 7, it is a world that can be better explored with this type of console.

You can just press a button on the console to start the broadcast on Twitch, applying these steps:

1. Press the share button on the PS4 controller when you are in the game.
2. Choose "Retransmit GamePlay".
3. Select the option to log in.
   4. Log on to https://twitch.tv/active to enter the code on the TV screen.
5. Choose OK via PS4.
6. Select Twitch once again.
7. Choose the options to start the transmission.
8. Stay live on Twitch.

When you want to end the transmission just press the option in the "Share" menu, there is also an application on Twitch on PS4, but it is not mandatory, only favors to see the transmissions of other people, that way you can find the transmissions on other video applications such as Netflix, HBO Go and on the PlayStation Store.

How it is possible to stream on Twitch via Nintendo Switch

Each existing console allows you to share the game by streaming, through Nintendo Switch you can find a high compatibility with Twitch services, it happens in the same way in which it is done through the PS4, and Xbox One, this is due to the variety of tools available for live streaming.

From the console itself you can take control of the broadcast, via Nintendo Switch this is possible, only the procedure is done the old-fashioned way, as you must use a capture card, they are simple steps actually, the important thing is that you can make the connection with the capture card to start exploiting the content on Twitch.

Playing live is a reality through Twitch, you just have to execute the following steps to stream:

- Get a capture card, since the Nintendo Switch does not work or does not support internal transmission as with other consoles of the modern generation, so you should bet on an external capture device, it is normal to invest in El-gato HD60, has an approximate cost of $ 200 USD. You can also find more versions of the capture card that will facilitate the transmission through high resolutions, but it is an additional expense.

- Once you have invested in obtaining the capture card, the next thing to do is to connect it to the base of the Switch and the TV, because it is the only way to transmit the video, so the card must be included in the HDMI output port of the dock, so you just have to press the specific switch, although you may need another HDMI cable to the TV to see what you are doing while you are transmitting.

- Connect the Elgato to a PC, you are going to require the functions of a PC, it must be close so it can be connected to the USB cable, plus the mini USB 2.0 port on the capture card, and the other end you can incorporate into the PC, that way you will be able to control the transmission software on the PC, but the image displayed is minimally delayed.

The HDMI connection that goes to the TV, displays the game in full without any delays, you must download the capture software to freely use the capture card, the advantage is that the PC does not have to function as a power source, as the capture card hardware receives most of the load.

Additionally, you should concentrate on having a stable internet connection, especially when transmitting, so it is best to use a wired internet connection to proceed with the steps:

- Create an account on the Twitch platform, if you already have an account you only need to take one simple step in the game, but if you don't you can complete each of the free steps.

- Link Twitch account with Elgato software, for this you can choose Twitch as the live streaming platform over Elgato software, that way you can log in and authorize the software to access your account. The Elgato software has everything you need for live streaming, although the features available may not be enough for you.

- You can also get the streaming software from third parties, so you can cover more control over the streaming, you can use free services such as OBS or XSplit, so you have the video capture functions of Elgato, as well as other options for streaming or recording videos.

Learn how to stream on Twitch using a laptop

Gaming streams to gaming platforms like Twitch and YouTube are a high trending event, so when you are looking to stream for your friends or social networks you can plan appropriate media with a well-rounded audience that can be built under a progressive process, but you are sure to wonder if you should invest too much.

The process to transmit is simple, by means of a laptop this becomes a reality, that is the way to start, you just need to know the minimum software and hardware requirements for you to use your computer for this purpose, as it is a way that works and you can use to your advantage to combine or use as input hardware.

The requirements that you must overcome for this is to have a CPU that is Intel Core i5-4670, or one that is equivalent to AMD, in the same way the level of memory matters since it must be 8 GB DDR3 SDRAM, with a Windows 7 Home Premium system, where you must mostly prioritize the requirement of the CPU for being the most important component.

The transmission process also depends on the age of the computer, as does the CPU speed, so with the i5-4670 you have a Haswell CPU of at least 3.4 GHz, those CPUs in computers are usually slower, as they suffer certain restrictions due to heat and power.

But those qualities are not an exclusive reason to perform transmission, as long as the proper configuration is practiced, the first step is the selection of additional hardware, because starting from the assertion that a laptop is able to meet a whole series of requirements for transmission, you must cover other points.

You can not neglect the issue of sound, for this it is best to bet on an external microphone, this is important so that viewers do not get faults or complaints, the same goes for the graphics these must overcome the low quality, without losing the fluidity of a compressed broadcast so that there is no point delayed.

These hardwares should be a help to offer attractive commentaries, with the best possible quality so that no user can get bored or withdraw from the broadcast, since some basic microphones that come integrated to the PC or headphones can fall far short of expectations.

Most streamers bet on the use of Blue Yeti, because it works as a full microphone, thus covering more than 90% of the audio in each transmission, if you have little budget you can opt for SnowBall, where you can offer a compact audio type, for half the price, it is acceptable.

The use of this kind of microphones every time you have to transmit facilitates the entire transmission process, also as long as they are elements that can be used via USB connection, everything is facilitated at your disposal to take with you wherever you want that study.

The essential thing is that the sound is not affected by any hardware problem, you can try with any devices you want as long as it is external, the next thing to try or cover is the internet connection, it may be something silly, but the recommended measure that you should seek to cover is the minimum 2 Mbps bandwidth load to transmit in 720p.

A useful tip is to opt for the wired connection, so that you have stability over the network, because WiFi suffers more alterations that can fragment your transmission, but it all depends on the degree of confidence you have about your internet connection, which corresponds to the software can be covered with different alternatives.

One software measure you can implement is Nvidia's Ge-Force Experience Share, as well as the premium options known as XSplit, but the usual is to use OBS; Open Broadcaster Software, this is totally free, and its functions are part of the open source quality.

Using these tools allows you to have a balanced performance, it is also easy to carry out any kind of configuration, to have more possibilities to make transmissions without problems, especially because OBS is at your disposal just by turning it on because you have all the scenes you need.

The ease of having a main scene such as a game, mixing explanation images, the projection of your face by the webcam, and the audio input through the microphone, is a simplicity that is exposed on a single screen, where you do not lose control to make any cut and then resume.

On each scene you can use a wide variety of sources, as well as a diversity of organizations, with a kind of simple placement so you do not overlook anything, in case you want to add an audio input device such as a microphone just press on the "+" sign.

This process is repeated with each type of software, so it is called a simple way in theory, the menu allows you to change and integrate seamlessly, where you should not miss the source that will help you to integrate the screenshot, this in turn allows you to change and create the scenes of the game that are more striking.

To carry out this process you must use the transmission key, to save all the settings and simply indicate to start the streaming, and everything you can continue to monitor by preview, in case you want to test what a transmission to your PC demands you can start the transmission with a "?", so that the transmission is sent, but it is not displayed on the channel, and thus you can detect failures.

When you find yourself streaming through the OBS software, you may compromise some of your PC resources, this can be reduced through the video options, so that you can lower the quality of the streaming output, you can set 720p as an acceptable size, and use the 30 frames per second speed.

Another setting you can change is the priority setting, instead of high, you can go to the advanced section of the configuration, other preset details can be chosen for slow CPUs, even the hardware coding can be changed for better results.

But you should not limit all the functions for the software to work properly, although disabling the preview is another way that can help you not to consume so many resources, what you should think about is to cover more power to the transmissions as the account progresses.

The issue of performance has many sides, because many prefer a gaming computer, and others with a decent computer can get by with the transmissions, it all depends on how you feel better working, so it is best to go testing until you take the final step in the transmissions.

- **Dell XPS 13 with Intel HD Graphics**

When thinking about streaming over a laptop, the addition of Intel HD graphics can cause curiosity and controversy, mostly because it may require a higher dose of patience, because the lack of graphics is a drawback for hardware coding and GPU, because it saturates 100% for any game.

Depending on the game and the type of streaming you do, you can start testing with 720p, that way you will be working with one of the lowest settings, this opportunity helps you to adapt to the capacity of the equipment, but still averaging how much fps you are able to cover, that way you can see how much it is affected.

When you manage to have a light CPU, you can have a laptop capable of playing and transmitting, imposing the limits of 30 fps that it is able to tolerate, this causes that no interruptions arise during transmission, but what does happen is that you notice the video compression on some scenes, but considering the level, it is acceptable.

It is necessary to experiment with graphic resources and invest, because in that way the broadcasts gain the value you expect to attract the attention of the audience, so that you don't have to apply a later understanding or much less.

- **Xiaomi Pro - Nvidia MX150**

It is known as a Xiaomi Pro Ultrabook that has an i5-8250U quality CPU, in addition to having four cores, and 8 GB of RAM, in terms of graphics it has Nvidia MX150, that way you are going to have a driver that is able to exceed your expectations, the MX150 is intended for a mobile version by the GT 1030.

This kind of quality offers what any GPU can't integrate, all this is on a totally thin Ultrabook, this access means that you can use the hardware coding to provide a good quality of transmission, and allows you to raise the quality of your own content as high as you want.

In all graphics options it provides 1080p quality, this performance is matched by a similar 720p performance, although the viewer receives a better experience on the stream, without any compression skip, so a 60 fps setting is accepted without any limitation or noticeable during the scenes.

Using an Ultrabook with a dedicated low-end GPU is sufficient to respond to 720p transmissions, so that the streaming can be displayed in high quality, with optimized performance.

- **The use of laptops designed for video games**

You can try with some computers that are oriented to support games, as this guarantees a better response, also they are computers that support all types of updates, the space for transmission is ensured by means of good equipment that has power.

Some computers that you can try with full recommendation is the GL62M-7REX, although it can offer a low transmission, if compared to a computer that has a mid-range GPU and is modern, for this reason to transmit from a laptop, you can find different alternatives to make this easier and easier.

In addition, you have the use of free software to fulfill any broadcasting purpose, and with a low configuration, along with the function of some hardware, you can obtain brilliant results so that you can broadcast a correct image to your community.

Tips for capturing epic moments on Twitch

Watching any Twitch channel is a synonym of finding some part of the content that you would like to share or that is shocking, no matter what the reason that catches your attention you can take a screenshot to share those kind of special moments or scenes, this is simple and it is becoming popular.

The clips function that Twitch has makes this easier, because just by pressing a few clicks, you can expose the most shocking of any channel you have seen, but it is a modality that has the channels with subscription, in the case of having clips, you must know the correct way to use them by following these steps:

1. Place the Twitch channel you have chosen, then check if it has the clips option available, because it is limited for some accounts, to check you must look for the purple subscription button to start, also clips can be obtained on live content, and it does not work with pre-recorded content.

2. Move the cursor over the video player, so that you click on the clip icon, by means of the lower right side, that way a 30 second video clip starts in a new tab, depending on the Twitch mode, you have up to 25 seconds before to capture since you have clicked and 5 seconds after.

3. Click on the tab so that you can view the clip you just recorded, then you can use and take advantage of the buttons of some social networks like Twitter, Facebook and Reddit to share the content, or you can copy the link and send it, once they watch the clip, users can see your name at the top and to save the clip, you can right click and select "save video as".

How to build an audience on your Twitch account

Twitch has a striking number of celebrities, as it is a platform that offers a way to monetize and develop content like no other, this modality and freedom to carry out a streaming is something that fans of this type of content were asking for, where an elegant style and diversity of themes is maintained.

The best streamers are dedicated to their accounts with a high professional level, but what users love the most is their personality to tell some content or develop it, so there is still room for many accounts, as long as you dedicate yourself to offer originality and a different way of telling that topic.

The profile you must meet to form a community, is that of a streamer who is humble, friendly, and above all who devotes much attention to the interaction, because the treatment that you emit in the chat has an important value for any community, so it is a duty to treat people as the most valuable of the account.

But the growth of the audience also has to do with the components or details of transmission, this has the name of meeting the; Opportunity, Presence, Interaction, Consistency and Ability, these are the points on which you must concentrate to create a real name.

In Twitch you can go very far, especially when you exhaust all the options to grow as it is to form some partnership, plus you can eventually provide users with some benefits to create a monthly subscription, which creates exclusivity and at the same time is a sign or symbol of income for you.

No matter what level of streamer you are, you should aim to improve, and put into practice all the actions that are trending in this medium, you can take into account these recommendations to make your account scale:

- **Find and define your niche**

To stand out in an environment with 2 million streamers, the first basic step you must take is to generate a good idea or theme, which at the same time must be different from the rest, because it is probably already being dealt with by another account, so you must specialize in something specific that you can transmit.

Although any theme you choose, must be completely mastered by you, so you can develop quality content, to gain the appreciation of viewers and convey that they count on you, you need to spread fun, laughter, entertainment and above all interest for them to continue watching you, all this under the naturalness.

- **Be constant**

It is vital that you keep your account under consistency, because that way users will treat you and schedule you as if you were a TV show, so every time you are going to be live, you can create a schedule, so it will be easy to promote it and users will remember to watch it without having to see the advertising.

- **Builds alliances**

A big part of the success of streamers are partnerships, because it is a way to share and multiply the sense of humor, it also raises the interaction of users because both communities are merged, so having a stream with someone with notable achievements or even with a celebrity on your topic, attracts a high level of traffic.